Making More Doughnuts

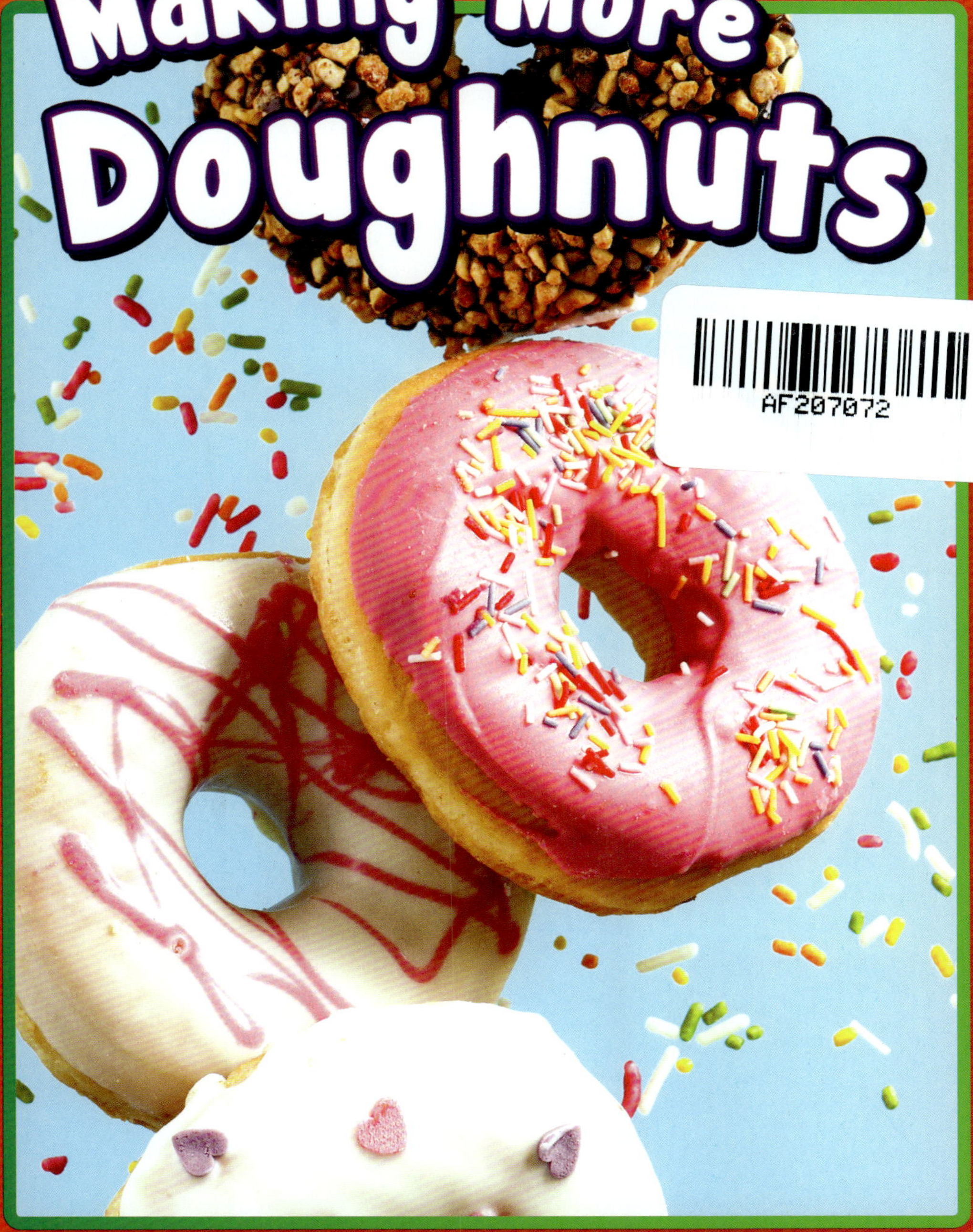

Anne Montgomery

Smithsonian

We love doughnuts!
They taste great!

People have loved
doughnuts for a long time.

4

They used to make them
at home.

6

Then, bakers made them.
Everyone wanted some!

Bakers made more. They used machines to do it.

BROOKLYN
TUBE CO.

People wanted more!
They made new machines.

Kreme

They made stores just
for doughnuts.

14

RANDY'S
DONUTS

We still love doughnuts!

STEAM CHALLENGE

The Problem

Your town bakers need a new shape for their doughnuts. They want your help.

The Goals

- Your doughnut should be a good shape and size to hold and eat.
- It should be made from play clay.
- Your doughnut should be held easily.

1 Research and Brainstorm

Learn about doughnuts.

2 Design and Build

Draw your plan. Make your doughnut shape!

3 Test and Improve

Hold your doughnut shape in your hands. Then, try to make it better.

4 Reflect and Share

What did you learn?

Consultants

Amy Zoque
STEM Coordinator and Instructional Coach
Vineyard STEM School
Ontario Montclair District

Siobhan Simmons
Marblehead Elementary
Capistrano Unified School District

Publishing Credits

Rachelle Cracchiolo, M.S.Ed., *Publisher*
Conni Medina, M.A.Ed., *Editor in Chief*
Diana Kenney, M.A.Ed., NBCT, *Series Developer*
Emily R. Smith, M.A.Ed., *Content Director*
Véronique Bos, *Creative Director*
Robin Erickson, *Art Director*
Stephanie Bernard, *Associate Editor*
Mindy Duits, *Series Designer*
Kevin Panter, *Senior Graphic Designer*
Smithsonian Science Education Center

Image Credits: p.5 Keystone Film Company/Wikipedia; p.7 Dick Whittington Studio/Corbis via Getty Images; p.9 Library of Congress [LC-A6199- 8541]; p.11 National Museum of American History; p.13 Jeffrey Greenberg/UIG via Getty Images; p.15 L. Pettet/iStock; all other images from iStock and/or Shutterstock.

Library of Congress Cataloging-in-Publication Data

Names: Montgomery, Anne (Anne Diana), author. | Smithsonian Institution.
Title: Making more doughnuts / Anne Montgomery.
Description: Huntington Beach, CA : Teacher Created Materials, [2019] |
  "Smithsonian Institution."-- Copyright statement. | Audience: Age 5. |
  Audience: K to grade 3. |
Identifiers: LCCN 2018055267 (print) | LCCN 2019000926 (ebook) | ISBN
  9781425859879 (eBook) | ISBN 9781493866427 (pbk.)
Subjects: LCSH: Doughnuts--Juvenile literature.
Classification: LCC TX770.D67 (ebook) | LCC TX770.D67 M66 2019 (print) | DDC
  641.8/653--dc23
LC record available at https://lccn.loc.gov/2018055267

Smithsonian

© 2019 Smithsonian Institution. The name "Smithsonian"
and the Smithsonian logo are registered trademarks
owned by the Smithsonian Institution.

Teacher Created Materials

5301 Oceanus Drive
Huntington Beach, CA 92649-1030
www.tcmpub.com
ISBN 978-1-4938-6642-7

© 2019 Teacher Created Materials, Inc.
Printed in China
51497

20